SPIRITUAL WARFARE PRAYERS FOR WOMEN

Modern Edition

30 Days Spiritual Warfare Prayer Book for Women.

Overcome Overthinking, Loneliness, Anger, Spiritual Attacks and Protection from Spiritual Darkness and so much More With God's Word.

Prayer Rocks

Table of Contents

Introduction
Welcome to the Battle

You're not here by accident.

I know you feel it—the weariness deep within, the heaviness pressing upon your spirit, the subtle whisper urging you to just give up. Perhaps it's the nagging doubt, or fear that creeps into your heart, the discouragement and confusion that leave you feeling isolated and weary. Sister, let me assure you, these battles you're facing are not mere coincidences, nor are they yours alone.

The reality is that we are at war. Not a war fought with weapons of flesh, but a fierce, spiritual battle fought on the battleground of our hearts and minds. The bible reminds us:

"For we do not wrestle against flesh and blood, but against principalities, against powers, against the rulers of the darkness of this age." (Ephesians 6:12 NKJV)

My beloved sister, God has led you to this prayer book for a reason—He sees you, He knows your struggles, and He desires your victory even more than you do. He has promised you strength in the midst of the storm, healing in your wounded places, and victory through the power of Christ. You are not here by accident. Rather, you are being positioned by the Lord Himself to experience breakthrough, healing, and the promised victory that is yours as a daughter of the Most High.

Together, we are going to embark on a powerful, Spirit-led journey. Over these next 30 days, you will learn to recognize the enemy's tactics, stand your ground in faith, and claim the promises that belong to you as a child of God.

"But thanks be to God, who gives us the victory through our Lord Jesus Christ." (1 Corinthians 15:57 NKJV)

Through Christ, victory is assured. Hold this truth tightly as we journey together.

How This Book Helps You: "From Battles to Breakthroughs: Your Clear Path to God's Promises"

Struggles	Your Actions	God's Promises
• Overthinking	• Pray Regularly	• Peace
• Loneliness	• Meditate Scripture	• Comfort
• Anger	• Build Community	• Protection
• Spiritual Attacks	• Forgive	• Strength
• Spiritual Darkness	• Practice Gratitude	• Clarity
• Anxiety	• Exercise Faith	• Restoration
• Fear	• Surrender to God	• Healing
• Temptation		

Life can feel challenging, and as women, we often face struggles like anxiety, loneliness, fear, anger, and even spiritual attacks. But there's good news: you're not alone in these battles.

This book clearly guides you through each struggle you face, showing you exactly what **you can do**— simple yet powerful actions like prayer, forgiving others, meditating on God's Word, or leaning on your community.

When you faithfully do your part, God promises incredible blessings in return—**peace, comfort, strength, clarity, and complete healing.** Each chapter and prayer in this book helps you move from your struggles to these beautiful breakthroughs.

Simply put, this book helps you understand:

Struggle ➜ Your Action (Prayer and Faith) ➜ God's Promised Breakthrough

By following this clear pathway, you'll not only find relief from life's difficulties, but you'll also step confidently into the joyful and victorious life God has promised you.

.

How to Use This Book

Think of these next 30 days as a purposeful walk with the Holy Spirit. Each day offers:

A Prayer: Begin each morning by reading the day's prayer aloud or silently. Invite the Holy Spirit to move in your heart, ask Him to center your thoughts on Christ, and welcome His protection and guidance.

Declaration: Around midday—or whenever you can steal a quiet moment—reflect on the day's theme and declare all you want to see in your life. Perhaps journal a few thoughts, voice a quick prayer, or pause to reorient your mind toward God's promises.

Scripture: The Word of God is your sword (Ephesians 6:17). Each day includes a passage or verses that will strengthen your faith. Let these Scriptures sink deeply into your spirit—memorize a line or two if you can, or replay them in your mind whenever worry tries to creep back in.

Evening Gratitude: Finally, close each evening with thankfulness. From the simplest blessings—like a place to lay your head—to the profound gift of God's grace in Christ, gratitude softens our hearts and draws us nearer to our Father.

If you miss a day, do not let guilt take root. Pick up where you left off, trusting that Jesus's mercies are new every morning (Lamentations 3:22–23).

Understanding Spiritual Warfare

Spiritual warfare is more than just a dramatic phrase; it's the daily reality of every believer. The apostle Paul urges us to "be strong in the Lord and in the power of His might," putting on the full armor of God so we can stand against the enemy's schemes (Ephesians 6:10–11).

Why It Matters: The Bible teaches that the devil prowls like a roaring lion, seeking whom he may devour (1 Peter 5:8). His tactics are deceit, accusation, and fear. But fear does not have the final say—Jesus does.

Where the Battle Rages: Although we see tensions in our daily circumstances—relationships, finances, health—Paul clarifies the true fight is spiritual. We engage in prayer, wield God's Word (Hebrews 4:12), and take captive every thought that opposes Christ's truth (2 Corinthians 10:3–5).

How We Stand Firm: We do not stand on our own strength. We stand in Jesus's victory. On the cross, He broke the power of sin and death (Colossians 2:14–15). Therefore, we do not wrestle for victory; we wrestle *from* victory. With the helmet of salvation secure and the sword of the Spirit in hand, we resist the enemy, confident in our rightful position as daughters of the King.

Over the next 30 days, you'll see how God's faithfulness, wisdom, and power bring healing to wounded places, triumph over dark lies, and breakthrough in seemingly impossible situations. Be encouraged to draw near to Him each day—and know that He has already won the war for your soul. These pages are a companion, but the Holy Spirit is your true guide.

With a heart of faith, approach each day expecting God to speak to you personally, to mend the broken pieces, and to breathe fresh life into dreams you thought were long gone. You are *not* alone in this journey. You have sisters around the world and throughout history who've stood where you stand now, and—by the grace of God—have come out singing on the other side.

So welcome, Sis. Take a deep breath, lift your eyes to the One who holds your future, and step into the next 30 days believing that our God can do exceedingly, abundantly more than you ask or imagine (Ephesians 3:20). Victory is on the horizon, and the Lord is faithful to see you through every battle you face.

"Now may the God of peace . . . equip you with everything good to do His will. And

may He accomplish in us what is pleasing
in His sight, through Jesus Christ, to whom
be glory forever and ever." —Hebrews
13:20–21 (adapted)

Welcome to the battle, dear sister, where together we'll discover the power of prayer, the comfort of Scripture, and the unwavering hope we find in Jesus. The Lord has gone before you, and He holds you in the palm of His hand.

Section 1: Laying the Foundation

"The thief does not come except to steal, and to kill, and to destroy. I have come that they may have life, and that they may have it more abundantly."
(John 10:10 NKJV)

Listen closely, sister: **the enemy** of your soul did not knock politely on the door of your heart—he broke in. He snuck through doubt, discouragement, or heartbreak and has tried to dismantle your peace, your joy, and your sense of worth. You may feel the weight of regret or the sting of insecurity. You may be fighting battles in your marriage, your motherhood, your finances, or even in your mind. But the truth is **you were never meant to fight alone.**

The day you said "yes" to Jesus, a powerful exchange took place: your old, sin-weary self was replaced by **a woman clothed in grace**, chosen by God to walk in the victory Jesus secured at the cross. You are a daughter of the King—transferred from the kingdom of darkness into **the kingdom of His marvelous light** (1 Peter 2:9). Yet if you do not lay hold of the spiritual resources God gives, the enemy will continue to test your defenses at every turn.

This section—**Laying the Foundation**—is like a spiritual blueprint: You'll discover how to anchor your identity in Christ, learn why prayer is our lifeline in warfare, and finally, see how God's armor protects you daily from the devil's schemes. Because, sister, **God's plan was never for you to cower.** His plan is for you to stand victorious in the authority and love He's bestowed on you.

Let's begin by setting our feet on the bedrock truth of who we are in Jesus, then pressing into the power of prayer, and finally dressing ourselves head-to-toe in God's armor. The enemy may threaten, but he cannot triumph over the woman who truly knows who she is, Whose she is, and the power she wields through prayer and God's Word.

1. OUR IDENTITY IN CHRIST

Why Knowing Who We Are in Jesus Is Our First Line of Defense...

"Therefore, if anyone is in Christ, he is a new creation; old things have passed away; behold, all things have become new."
(2 Corinthians 5:17 NKJV)

For many of us, the struggles in our lives—whether past abuse, ongoing guilt, crippling fears, or self-doubt—begin with a distorted sense of who we are. When we don't grasp our true identity in Christ, the enemy finds footholds in our insecurity and shame. He whispers accusations: *"You're not good enough. You're too damaged. God won't help someone like you."*

But here is **God's definitive answer** to every one of those lies: **"In Christ, you are a new creation**—redeemed, chosen, loved, and forgiven" (Ephesians 1:7; 1 Peter 2:9). Your identity is not in your past mistakes or your present challenges; your identity is in the finished work of Jesus. The very moment you accepted Christ, you moved from *orphan* to *daughter*, from *condemned* to *fully pardoned*, from *broken* to *beloved*.

How This Identity Protects Us

1. Confidence Instead of Shame

Satan's oldest trick is to convince believers they must still live in condemnation for past sins. But Romans 8:1 boldly proclaims, "There is therefore now no condemnation for those who are in Christ Jesus." When you stand on this promise, shame loses its grip and your confidence in God's love takes root.

2. Authority Over the Enemy

Believers in Christ have been given authority to "trample on serpents and scorpions" (Luke 10:19)—a vivid picture of standing victorious over demonic attacks. The devil thrives where ignorance reigns, but when you **know** you are seated in heavenly places with Christ (Ephesians 2:6), you can pray and resist the enemy from a place of triumph rather than fear.

3. A Present and Future Hope

Your worth is no longer based on fleeting achievements or the acceptance of others. It rests securely in the unchanging grace of God. Like the royal daughter you are, you can lift your head high, recognizing that He who began a good work in you will complete it (Philippians 1:6).

Reflection

- **Where in your life do you feel most unworthy or ashamed?** Bring that to the foot of the cross. Remember, your identity is in Christ's righteousness, not your performance.
- **What lies about yourself have you been tempted to believe?** Ask the Holy Spirit to replace these lies with Scriptures that affirm your identity.

2. THE POWER OF PRAYER

"The effective, fervent prayer of a righteous man avails much." *(James 5:16 NKJV)*

Prayer is **your spiritual heartbeat**, the lifeline that ties your spirit to God's. When we pray, we aren't merely sending hopeful thoughts into the universe; we are **communing with the Almighty**, the One who spoke the world into existence.

God invites His daughters to come boldly (Hebrews 4:16). Not timidly, not with a sense of unworthiness, but boldly—convinced that the Lord hears us and loves to respond to our petitions. Through prayer, we break free from the enemy's illusions of helplessness and access the immeasurable power of God.

Connecting to Heaven's Power

1. Shift of Focus

When you pray, your focus shifts from the problems on earth to the unshakable throne of God. Fear, anxiety, and hopelessness begin to bow in His presence. He reminds you that **He** is bigger than any storm.

2. **Deepening of Faith**

Prayer is not a last-ditch effort; it's an ongoing conversation that strengthens your faith day by day. As you present every care to God (1 Peter 5:7), you also begin to witness His faithfulness—sometimes in immediate answers, other times in gentle guidance that sustains you through difficulties.

3. **Direct Resistance to Darkness**

When faced with spiritual attacks—thoughts of condemnation, patterns of sin, or even demonic oppression—prayer becomes a **battle cry**. James 4:7 commands, "Resist the devil and he will flee from you." We resist him **in prayer**, declaring God's truth over the lies that bombard our minds.

Practical Prayer Habits for Every Woman

- **Morning Surrender**

Before the chaos of the day ensues, spend a few moments surrendering your plans, your worries, and your victories to the Lord.

- **Midday Check-In**

Pause at midday to recalibrate your heart. Whisper short prayers of gratitude or intercession for others.

- **Evening Thanksgiving**

End your day recounting God's faithfulness. Reflect on how He walked with you, and place all burdens back into His hands.

3. THE ARMOR OF GOD

"Finally, be strong in the Lord and in the power of His might. Put on the whole armor of God, that you may be able to stand against the wiles of the devil." *(Ephesians 6:10–11 NKJV)*

The moment you wake each day, forces beyond what you can see are at work to discourage, distract, and defeat you. But God, in His great love, has not left you defenseless. He's given you **spiritual armor** that guards your mind, protects your heart, and empowers you to victoriously engage in warfare.

a. Belt of Truth

The belt secured every other part of the Roman soldier's armor. Likewise, the truth of God's Word secures our entire spiritual defense.

- **For Women**: When the enemy whispers lies—*"You'll always be alone," "Your past defines you"—anchor yourself in God's unchanging truth. Let Scripture be your standard, not shifting emotions or opinions.

b. Breastplate of Righteousness

This piece protected a soldier's vital organs, especially the heart. Righteousness—the righteousness of Christ—guards your most vulnerable self.

- **For Women**: Shame and guilt often attack our hearts, telling us we're unworthy or beyond hope. But through faith in Christ, we wear **His righteousness**, shielding our hearts from accusation.

c. Shoes of Peace

Roman soldiers' sandals had nails or spikes to ensure firm footing, especially on rough terrain. We likewise stand firm on the **gospel of peace**.

- **For Women**: Busyness and stress can rob our peace—whether in caring for family, navigating careers, or battling anxiety. Clothe your feet with peace by **trusting** in God's sovereignty. Let His calm carry you through life's storms.

d. Shield of Faith

A shield protects from fiery darts—ambushes that come unexpectedly. Our faith in God's promises quenches every arrow of the enemy.

- **For Women**: Faith is not blind optimism; it's **active trust** in the One who never fails. When fear strikes—over finances, children's futures, marital struggles—hold up your shield of faith, refusing to bow to fear's threats.

e. Helmet of Salvation

The helmet protects the mind—where battles are most often waged. Salvation secures us in Christ's victory.

- **For Women**: Negative self-talk, comparison, or condemnation can take root in our thoughts. Renew your mind daily (Romans 12:2). Remind yourself of the **saving grace** that positions you as God's beloved daughter.

f. Sword of the Spirit

The only offensive weapon—a sharp, double-edged sword—represents the **Word of God**.

- **For Women**: Your power to tear down lies and stand against temptation is **Scripture**. Speak it out loud in prayer. Declare verses over your life, your home, and every challenge. God's Word in your mouth is a force the enemy cannot withstand.

Sister, **you are fully known and fiercely loved** by the Creator of the universe. You are chosen and called to stand strong in His might. When you know who you are in Christ, cultivate a vibrant prayer life, and clothe yourself with God's armor daily, you become a woman the enemy dreads to see rise each morning.

This foundation—your identity, the power of prayer, and the protective armor you wear—positions you to see **breakthroughs, healing, and victory**. Let these truths sink deep. Embrace them wholeheartedly. And remember:

"In all these things we are more than conquerors through Him who loved us." *(Romans 8:37 NKJV)*

Take heart. Stand firm. Your victory in Christ is **assured**. Now let's learn to walk it out, day by day, wearing the armor and wielding the authority that belongs to every daughter of the King.

Section 2: 30 Days of Spiritual Warfare Prayers for Women

In this 30-day journey, you will discover the transforming power of prayer, God's Word, and purposeful declarations as you stand firm in victory. Brace yourself—your mighty Champion fights beside you. Today is the day to lift your head, roll up your sleeves, and advance boldly. The King of Kings is on your side!

Day 1 – Overcoming Anxiety and Worry

Key Scripture

"Do not be anxious about anything, but in every situation, by prayer and petition, with thanksgiving, present your requests to God. And the peace of God, which transcends all understanding, will guard your

hearts and your minds in Christ Jesus."
(Philippians 4:6–7)

Devotional Thought

Anxiety often creeps into our hearts through
seemingly small concerns: an unexpected bill, a
child's health scare, and uncertainty about the
future. When these nagging worries accumulate, we
may feel suffocated by a fog of fear. But Jesus invites
us to bring every anxious thought to Him. Each time
we offload our cares onto the Lord, we make room
for His peace to take charge of our minds. The Holy
Spirit gently reminds us that worry is a burden we
were never meant to carry. Hand it all over in prayer,
and step into the calm your loving Father has
prepared.

Prayer Focus

- **Release of Anxiety**: Ask God to search
  your heart and reveal any hidden anxieties.
  Surrender each one at His feet.

- **Infusion of Peace**: Invite the Holy Spirit to flood every corner of your mind with the peace that surpasses all understanding.

Prayer:

Heavenly Father, I _____ come to You with every anxious thought weighing me down. Today, I cast each care into Your loving hands, believing You care for me. I ask for Your peace to replace my worry. I thank You that I do not stand alone in this battle; Your presence is my strong tower. In Jesus' Name, amen.

Declaration

"I declare that fear has no permanent hold on me. God's peace guards my heart and mind. I will rest in His promises, for He is faithful."

Journaling Prompt

Reflect on a specific concern that's been weighing on you. Write down how you sense God inviting you to rest, trust, and breathe deeply in His presence.

Day 1

Date: _____

_____
_____
_____
_____
_____
_____
_____
_____
_____
_____
_____
_____
_____
_____
_____
_____
_____
_____
_____
_____

Day 2 – Breaking Generational Curses

Key Scripture

"...for I, the Lord your God, am a jealous God, punishing the children for the sin of the parents... but showing love to a thousand generations of those who love me and keep my commandments." *(Exodus 20:5–6)*

Devotional Thought

We all inherit some form of spiritual "baggage" from our family lines—habits, mindsets, and patterns that can feel impossible to shake. But the beauty of the gospel is that Jesus Christ breaks every chain, including generational iniquities that have lingered for years. A new bloodline—His—flows through you, offering a fresh legacy of hope, holiness, and freedom for you and those who come after you.

Prayer Focus

- **Identification of Patterns**: Ask the Holy Spirit to pinpoint any repeated destructive patterns in your family line—whether addiction, anger, unbelief or something else.
- **Declaration of Freedom**: In Christ, boldly renounce any inherited strongholds, inviting God's mercy and a fresh family legacy.

Praycr:

Mighty Deliverer, I _____ confess that certain destructive cycles have plagued my family line. Today, I stand on the blood of Jesus Christ, which speaks a better word than any curse. I plead the victory of Calvary over myself, my household, and my lineage. I declare a new legacy of righteousness, peace, and blessing—starting now. In the powerful Name of Jesus, amen.

Declaration

"My family's future is rooted in Christ, not in the failures of the past. I break every chain by the power of Jesus' blood, and I welcome a new era of blessing."

Journaling Prompt

Where in your life do you sense repeating, unhealthy patterns? Write a short prayer that seals your decision to break free and walk in God's blessing for future generations.

Day 2

Date: _____

_____
_____
_____
_____
_____
_____
_____
_____
_____
_____
_____
_____
_____
_____
_____
_____
_____
_____
_____
_____

Day 3 – Healing from Heartbreak and Hurt

Key Scripture

"He heals the brokenhearted and binds up their wounds." *(Psalm 147:3)*

Devotional Thought

Heartbreak can come from betrayal, strained relationships, or life's bitter disappointments. Such wounds may run deep, making you feel fractured and forgotten. Yet God is the Healer of broken hearts. He collects your tears and knows your pain. This journey of healing might require time, tears, and surrender, but take courage: Jesus mends every broken piece with gentleness and love. He transforms scars into testimonies of His grace.

Prayer Focus

- **Acknowledgment of the Hurt**: Be honest before God about the depth of your pain.

- **Invitation for Healing**: Ask the Lord to pour the oil of His healing over those raw, hurting places, and to bring beauty from ashes.

Prayer:

Dear Jesus, You see me _____ In my shattered places and love me still. You are my Comforter, and I open my heart to You now. I ask for healing from hurts I can't fully articulate. I renounce bitterness and anger; instead, I invite Your gentle touch. Let Your compassion restore my soul and allow me to love freely again. In Your precious Name, amen.

Declaration

"I am not defined by past hurt. My heart is healing under the compassionate hand of God. My future is bright, and my scars will serve as proof of God's restoring power."

Journaling Prompt

Recall a time when you felt God's nearness in your pain. Record how that moment gave you hope for deeper healing in your present circumstances.

Day 3

_____

_____

_____

_____

_____

_____

_____

_____

_____

_____

_____

_____

_____

_____

_____

_____

_____

_____

_____

_____

_____

_____

Day 4 – Trials in Marriage

Key Scripture

"Love is patient, love is kind... It always protects, always trusts, always hopes, always perseveres. Love never fails." *(1 Corinthians 13:4–8)*

Devotional Thought

Marriage, whether you're living in its reality or praying for one in the future, requires grace, patience, and relentless perseverance. Conflict or disappointment in marriage can spur you to feel alone and misunderstood. Yet God calls you to navigate these trials with the kind of sacrificial love He demonstrates toward us daily. When He is at the center, your union can weather any storm. Even if you're waiting on marriage, let God shape your heart to love as He loves. Cling to His Word—He is your anchor.

Prayer Focus

- **Surrender Selfishness**: Ask God to reveal areas where self-focused thinking has overshadowed unity.
- **Release of Forgiveness**: Pray for divine enabling to offer and receive forgiveness, breaking cycles of resentment.

Prayer:

Lord, You designed marriage to reflect Your covenant love. Where there is discord, bring healing and unity. Where I have harbored anger or pride, forgive me. Teach me, _____, to love humbly and sacrificially, just as Christ loves the Church. I trust You to restore what has been fractured. In Jesus' Name, amen.

Declaration

"My marriage—or future marriage—is redeemed by the love of Christ. I choose unity, forgiveness, and sacrificial love. God's power is greater than any conflict."

Journaling Prompt

Write down one practical act of selfless love you can carry out for your spouse (or a future spouse) this week. Prayerfully commit to do it, trusting the Holy Spirit to strengthen you.

Day 4

Date: _____

_____

_____

_____

_____

_____

_____

_____

_____

_____

_____

_____

_____

_____

_____

_____

_____

_____

_____

_____

Day 5 – Confronting Addiction

Key Scripture

"No temptation has overtaken you except what is common to mankind. And God is faithful; he will not let you be tempted beyond what you can bear... he will also provide a way out." *(1 Corinthians 10:13)*

Devotional Thought

Addiction isn't limited to substances. Some of us feel chained to approval, shopping, food, social media— anything that consumes our hearts and displaces God from His rightful throne. It's time to recognize that we serve a God who breaks chains and sets captives free. His grace both forgives our past and empowers our future. Surrender your struggle to Him; His strength will shine in your weakness.

Prayer Focus

- **Expose the Lie**: Confess any addiction or dependency you've kept hidden, asking God to replace it with His truth.
- **Pursuit of Wholeness**: Pray for practical wisdom—such as accountability partners, professional help, or new habits—that aligns with your freedom.

Prayer:

God, You are my strength. Thank You that no temptation is greater than the power You have placed within me. Today, I, _____, renounce the grip of addiction in my life. Holy Spirit, fill every empty space and redirect my desires toward what is good, pure, and true. Give me the courage to reach out for help when I need it. I trust You completely to be my Deliverer. In Jesus' Name, amen.

Declaration

"I declare that no stronghold is too powerful for my God. I choose freedom over bondage, empowered by the Holy Spirit to walk in victory."

Journaling Prompt

List the triggers or situations that lead you into addictive behaviors. Ask the Lord for a strategy to overcome each trigger, and commit to one action step toward freedom.

Day 5   Date: _____

_____

_____

_____

_____

_____

_____

_____

_____

_____

_____

_____

_____

_____

_____

_____

_____

_____

_____

_____

Day 6 – Overcoming Sexual Sin (Adultery & Fornication)

Key Scripture

"It is God's will that you should be sanctified: that you should avoid sexual immorality; that each of you should learn to control your own body in a way that is holy and honorable." *(1 Thessalonians 4:3–4)*

Devotional Thought

Sexual sin can shroud your heart in shame and push you to hide from the very God who can heal you. Whether you've struggled with past mistakes or ongoing temptation, God's desire is to make you whole and holy. Sin's counterfeit promises will always fall short of the deep fulfillment found in Christ. Purity is not about condemnation; it's about stepping into the rich freedom and dignity God intends for His daughters.

Prayer Focus

- **Repentance and Cleansing**: Acknowledge any area where sexual sin has taken root, and turn to God for forgiveness.
- **Renewed Desires**: Pray for God to transform your mind, filling you with a passion for holiness and an ability to resist temptation.

Prayer:

Holy God, You created me, _____, for purity in both body and mind. I turn away from any sexual sin that has taken hold in my life, and I fully receive the forgiveness You so freely give. Strengthen me to resist temptation and walk in the freedom You designed for me. My body is a temple of the Holy Spirit, and I choose to honor You with it. Teach me to walk in dignity, self-control, and true holiness. In Jesus' Name, amen.

Declaration: "The blood of Jesus purifies me from all unrighteousness. I stand clothed in the righteousness of Christ. My mind, body, and spirit are consecrated to God."

Journaling Prompt: Write about what purity looks like for you in your current season of life. Ask God to reveal practical ways to guard your heart daily.

Day 6

_____

_____

_____

_____

_____

_____

_____

_____

_____

_____

_____

_____

_____

_____

_____

_____

_____

_____

Day 7 – Disarming Imposter Syndrome / Self-Doubt

Key Scripture

"…'My grace is sufficient for you, for my power is made perfect in weakness.' Therefore I will boast all the more gladly about my weaknesses, so that Christ's power may rest on me." *(2 Corinthians 12:9–10)*

Devotional Thought

Feeling like a fraud, or fearing you aren't good enough, can sabotage your confidence and cause you to shrink back from God's calling. But here's the truth: God's power shines through our frailties. It's never been about our flawless qualifications; it's about the Holy Spirit equipping us to fulfill His plan. When you confront self-doubt with faith, your perceived weaknesses become platforms for God's glory.

Prayer Focus

- **Renouncing Lies**: Identify the negative voices that whisper "You can't" or "You're not worthy," and break agreement with them in Jesus' Name.
- **Affirming God's Call**: Ask God for fresh confidence in the unique assignments He has placed in your life.

Prayer:

Lord, today I, _____, release every insecurity and self-imposed limitation I've held onto for too long. Forgive me for the times I've doubted the power You've placed within me. I reject every lie that says I'm not enough or unqualified. Instead, I embrace Your supernatural grace. Let Your strength be magnified in my weaknesses so that I may serve and glorify You boldly, without hesitation. In Jesus' mighty Name, amen.

Declaration

"I am chosen, called, and equipped by God. Imposter syndrome has no voice in my life. In Christ, I can do all things He ordains."

Journaling Prompt: List the lies that self-doubt has told you. Next to each, write out God's truth from Scripture that counters them (for example, replace "I'm not worthy" with "I am fearfully and wonderfully made," Psalm 139:14).

Day 7

Date: _____

_____

_____

_____

_____

_____

_____

_____

_____

_____

_____

_____

_____

_____

_____

_____

_____

_____

_____

_____

Day 8 – Facing Fear

"For God has not given us a spirit of fear, but of power and of love and of a sound mind." *(2 Timothy 1:7)*

Devotional Thought

Fear paralyzes faith. It robs you of bold prayer, bold love, and bold obedience. Yet Scripture reminds us that fear is not our inheritance—power, love, and a sound mind are! Courage is not the absence of fear; it is choosing to move forward in spite of it, trusting the God who fights for you. When you magnify God's promises above your frightening circumstances, fear loses its grip.

Prayer Focus

- **Confronting Fear**: Name the specific areas of dread or anxiety that have held you back, and lay them before the Lord.

- **Receiving God's Courage**: Pray for a renewed spirit of boldness to pursue your calling fearlessly.

Prayer:

Father, fear has tried to hold me captive, but today, I choose to stand on Your truth. I, _____, am not bound by fear, because You have given me a spirit of power, love, and a sound mind through the Holy Spirit. I refuse to be intimidated by the enemy's lies. I trust You completely to guide my steps as I walk in faith, not fear. In Jesus' Name, amen.

Declaration

"I reject every notion of fear, for my God is greater. I embrace the Holy Spirit's power and walk in love and clarity of mind."

Journaling Prompt

Reflect on a time when you overcame fear through God's help. How can you apply that same faith to your current situation?

Day 8

Date: _____

_____
_____
_____
_____
_____
_____
_____
_____
_____
_____
_____
_____
_____
_____
_____
_____
_____
_____
_____
_____
_____
_____

Day 9 – Loneliness and Isolation

Key Scripture

"God sets the lonely in families..." *(Psalm 68:6)*

Devotional Thought

Loneliness can strike in a room full of people or in the quietness of an empty home. While seasons of solitude can deepen our reliance on God, persistent isolation is not the Lord's plan. He longs to place each of us in communities—spiritual families— where we are known, nurtured, and loved. Even if your heart has been wounded by others, open it again to the people God brings into your life. You were designed for godly connections and friendships that echo His love.

Prayer Focus

- **Desire for Connection**: Ask God to break down walls—whether fear, hurt, or shame— that block intimacy with others.

- **Eyes to See Community**: Pray that the Holy Spirit guides you to the right friendships, mentors, or small groups that foster a sense of belonging.

Prayer:

Lord, You created me, _____, for connection. When I retreat into loneliness, draw me out with Your unfailing love. Surround me with people who encourage and strengthen my faith, and help me to be a source of love for those who feel alone. Thank You for always being with me, my closest companion. In Jesus' Name, amen.

Declaration

"I am never truly alone because God is always near. I choose to foster community and let His love flow through me to others."

Journaling Prompt

Identify one step you can take this week to reach out for deeper fellowship (sending a message, joining a

small group, or reconnecting with an old friend).
Write how you feel about that step and commit to act
on it.

Day 9

_____

_____

_____

_____

_____

_____

_____

_____

_____

_____

_____

_____

_____

_____

_____

_____

_____

_____

_____

Day 10 – Relationship Struggles (Friendships, Dating, and More)

Key Scripture

"Therefore, as God's chosen people... bear with each other and forgive one another... Forgive as the Lord forgave you." *(Colossians 3:12–13)*

Devotional Thought

Friendships can be complicated, dating can feel uncertain, and betrayal can cut deeper than we ever imagined. Broken trust creates walls that seem hard to tear down. Yet God calls us to be peacemakers, to set boundaries that reflect His holiness, and to respond with both truth and grace. Commit to letting God reshape your perspective: maintain healthy boundaries, speak truth in love, and extend compassion without enabling destructive behavior. He will guide you in relationships that honor Him.

Prayer Focus

- **Relational Wisdom**: Ask God for discernment on which relationships to cultivate and how to navigate conflict well.
- **Healing & Restoration**: Intercede for damaged connections, praying for the Holy Spirit to move hearts toward reconciliation, if at all possible.

Prayer:

Father, You have given me, _____, a heart that longs for healthy, meaningful relationships. When misunderstandings arise or hurt tries to take root, fill me with wisdom, truth, and a spirit of forgiveness. If any relationship has broken beyond my control, I trust You to restore it in Your perfect way and timing— if it is Your will. Heal what is wounded, rebuild trust where it has been shaken, and help me reflect Your love in every interaction. In Jesus' Name, amen.

Declaration: "My relationships belong to God. I choose patience, humility, and forgiveness, trusting the Lord to guard my heart and guide me into thriving friendships and connections."

Journaling Prompt: Think of a relationship where tension or misunderstanding has arisen. Write down how you feel God is prompting you to respond—whether through setting boundaries, offering forgiveness, or seeking wise counsel.

Day 10

_____

_____

_____

_____

_____

_____

_____

_____

_____

_____

_____

_____

_____

_____

_____

_____

_____

_____

_____

_____

_____

Day 11 – Breaking Strongholds of Sin

Key Scripture

"For the weapons of our warfare are not carnal but mighty in God for pulling down strongholds... bringing every thought into captivity to the obedience of Christ." *(2 Corinthians 10:4–5)*

Devotional Thought

Sometimes, it's not just one habitual sin but entrenched patterns of thinking and behavior that seem to imprison us. These strongholds can feel immovable, but God assures us that His power shatters them. When you deliberately align your thoughts with God's truth, the grip of sin loosens its hold. Allow the Holy Spirit to reveal any secret addictions or hidden attitudes of the heart, and let Him train you to stand firm with His Word as your mighty weapon.

Prayer Focus

1. **Recognition**: Ask God to expose any mindset or habit that has become a spiritual stronghold in your life.

2. **Captivity**: Surrender these thoughts and behaviors to Christ. Trust the Holy Spirit to renew your mind daily.

Prayer

Father, You have given me everything I need to stand strong. Right now, I, _____, lay down every thought that pulls me away from You. Show me where I've been trapped in patterns that do not honor You, and lead me into freedom. I surrender my mind to Your truth and ask for the strength to take every thought captive to Christ. By the authority of Jesus' Name, I stand in victory. Amen.

Declaration

"I declare I have the mind of Christ. All strongholds in my life crumble under the power of God's Word. I am free and victorious!"

Day 12 – Emotional Healing (Depression, Trauma, Grief)

Key Scripture

"He has sent me to bind up the brokenhearted... to comfort all who mourn... to give them beauty for ashes." *(Isaiah 61:1–3)*

Devotional Thought

Depression, trauma, and grief are heavy burdens that can cloud our days and steal our joy. But the One who designed your heart is the same One who mends it. He doesn't shy away from your tears. He sees the broken places that no one else can see and offers comfort that no one else can give. In His presence, you find true restoration—beauty in exchange for ashes.

Prayer Focus

1. **Release**: Offer every wounded area—memories, regrets, and sorrows—to the God who heals.

2. **Hope & Joy**: Ask the Holy Spirit to breathe new life and joy into places of despair.

Prayer

Jesus, You are my Healer and the One who lifts my head. Today, I, _____, bring You my pain—the losses, the wounds, the disappointments I carry. I lay them at Your feet, trusting You to bind up my brokenness. Where there is heaviness, fill me with hope. Where there is mourning, let Your joy take its place. I believe You are restoring what has been lost, and I choose to trust Your gentle hand. Amen.

Declaration

"I will not remain in the shadow of grief or trauma. My God heals my heart, and I shall walk in His promised joy."

Day 13 – Heart Posture: Honesty & Openness Before God

Key Scripture

"Behold, You desire truth in the innermost being…" (*Psalm 51:6*)

Devotional Thought

God longs for you to approach Him with authenticity—no masks, no pretenses, no hiding in shame. When you're candid about your struggles and failings, He draws close to bring healing. True freedom is found in confession and repentance. As you bare your soul, God responds not with condemnation, but with mercy and grace.

Prayer Focus

1. **Transparency**: Ask God for the courage to be real before Him, admitting struggles and shortcomings.

2. **Release of Shame**: Pray for the assurance of His love, even in the midst of brokenness.

Prayer

Father, I know there have been times when I, _____, have tried to hide my sin or my pain from You. But You see it all, and still, You call me to honesty and grace. So here I am, laying down my weaknesses and failures before You. Wash me clean, renew my heart, and restore the joy I once knew in You. Help me walk in Your truth every single day. In Jesus' Name, amen.

Declaration

"I am free to be honest with my God. He meets me with mercy, not judgment. My heart is open, and His grace abounds in me."

Day 14 – Rebuking Temptation

Key Scripture

"Submit yourselves therefore to God. Resist the devil, and he will flee from you." *(James 4:7)*

Devotional Thought

Temptation strikes us all: a whisper to lie, a pull toward compromise, a lustful thought that refuses to be silenced. Yet Scripture offers hope: If you stand firm in your submission to God, the devil's fiery darts lose their power. The Word of God is like a sword that cuts through deception, reminding you that you're not a victim but a conqueror in Christ. When you say "no" to the tempter, heaven backs you up.

Prayer Focus

1. **Resistance**: Ask the Holy Spirit for discernment to see temptation coming and resist it with Scripture.

2. **Victory Mindset**: Pray for strength to stand firm, believing God has already provided a way out.

Prayer

Today, I, _____, take a stand. I refuse to give in to temptations—whether they creep in quietly or come at me full force. I surrender my desires, my will, and my thoughts completely to You, God. Fill my heart with Your Word so deeply that when the enemy strikes, I will fight back with truth like a sharpened sword. Strengthen me to walk in victory, not for my own sake, but for Your glory. In the mighty Name of Jesus, amen.

Declaration

"I am not defenseless against temptation. I choose obedience over compromise. By God's power, the enemy must flee."

Day 15 – Finding Confidence in Christ

Key Scripture

"Have no fear of sudden disaster... for the Lord will be your confidence." *(Proverbs 3:25–26)*

Devotional Thought

In a culture of social media comparisons, many of us wrestle with self-doubt. True confidence doesn't stem from human applause or external status; it's rooted in who God says you are. When you remember that He's called and equipped you, you can step into every challenge with boldness—knowing it's His strength at work in you, not your own.

Prayer Focus

1. **Identity in Christ**: Ask God to remind you of the value and purpose He's placed on you.

2. **Courage**: Pray for boldness to pursue what God has set before you, rejecting fear of failure.

Prayer

Lord, thank You that my worth is secure in You. Tear down every lie that tells me I, _____, am not enough. Teach me to rest in the certainty of Your unfailing love. When I see impossibility, give me the courage to move forward, knowing You are right behind me. I refuse to compare myself to others—I choose instead to embrace the identity You have given me. In Jesus' Name, amen.

Declaration

"I am chosen, loved, and empowered by Christ. My confidence is unshakeable, for the Lord Himself undergirds me."

Day 16 – Healing from Abuse and Betrayal

Key Scripture

"I will restore to you the years that the swarming locust has eaten." *(Joel 2:25)*

Devotional Thought

Abuse and betrayal can shatter a person's sense of safety and trust. The scars left behind can feel impossible to heal. But the God who created you knows every tear and every moment of trauma. He promises to restore even the "lost years," to mend shattered hearts, and to redeem your story. As you open these wounds before Him, allow Him to pour in the oil of comfort and start you on a journey toward wholeness—emotionally and spiritually.

Prayer Focus

1. **Acknowledgment & Release**: Acknowledge the pain, and release it to God's capable hands.

2. **Redemption**: Ask God to rewrite your story, turning what was meant for harm into a testimony of His grace.

Prayer

Father of Compassion, You see the hidden wounds I, _____, carry. You know the pain, the trauma, and the betrayal that have left their mark on my heart. Today, I lay them before You, trusting in Your gentle healing. Uproot the bitterness and fear that have taken hold of me, and replace them with hope and purpose. Remind me that I am not defined by what happened to me, but by Your redeeming love. In Jesus' powerful Name, amen.

Declaration

"I will no longer be defined by abuse or betrayal. God is restoring my heart, rewriting my story, and bringing beauty out of the ruins."

Day 17 – Overcoming Bitterness and Unforgiveness

Key Scripture

"Get rid of all bitterness... forgiving each other, just as in Christ God forgave you." *(Ephesians 4:31–32)*

Devotional Thought

Bitterness is like a poison we drink, hoping to harm someone else. Yet it only harms our souls. Unforgiveness is a dead-end street that stunts spiritual growth and severs our intimacy with God. But when we remember the magnitude of God's forgiveness toward us, we're empowered to let go of offenses. Forgiveness is not a passive act—it's a powerful choice that sets us free.

Prayer Focus

1. **Confession**: Acknowledge the bitterness in your heart and ask for God's help to release it.

2. **Forgiveness**: Speak the names of those who've hurt you, and entrust them to God's mercy and justice.

Prayer

God of mercy, I, _____, acknowledge that bitterness has taken root in my heart. I don't want to carry this weight any longer. Right now, as an act of faith, I let go of every offense. I choose to forgive, just as You have forgiven me. Wash away the anger, heal the wounds, and fill me with a peace that goes beyond understanding. I am free from bitterness. In Jesus' Name, amen.

Declaration

"My soul is liberated through forgiveness. I release anger and resentment. God's love flows in me, granting wholeness and freedom."

Day 18 – Physical Health and Well-Being

Key Scripture

"I pray that you may enjoy good health and that all may go well with you, even as your soul is getting along well." *(3 John 1:2)*

Devotional Thought

Your body is a temple of the Holy Spirit, worthy of care and stewardship. Illness, chronic pain, or neglect can drain your spirit and make everyday tasks seem daunting. But God cares about your physical well-being. As you seek healing—through prayer, medical help, or lifestyle changes—remember that He is the One who knit you together. He's with you every step toward better health.

Prayer Focus

1. **Wholeness & Healing**: Lift up any specific health concerns, trusting God for intervention.

2. **Discipline & Wisdom**: Pray for self-control and a balanced lifestyle that honors God with your body.

Prayer

Lord, I _____ thank You for creating my body intricately. You know every cell and system. I ask for Your healing touch on any physical ailment I face. Grant me wisdom to make healthy choices and discipline to follow through. Where I feel weak, be my strength. May my body, mind, and spirit align with Your perfect will. In Jesus' Name, amen.

Declaration

"My body belongs to the Lord. By His wisdom and grace, I steward my health well. I trust God for strength, restoration, and vitality."

Day 19 – Generational Blessings

Key Scripture

"...He is the faithful God, keeping his covenant of love to a thousand generations..." *(Deuteronomy 7:9)*

Devotional Thought

Just as generational curses can pass down broken patterns, we can actively release generational blessings over our families. Whether you have children or not, your prayers can shape future generations, paving paths of faith, hope, and righteousness. God's covenant love stretches beyond our lifetime. As you pray blessings over your family, picture seeds of faith blossoming in those who follow after you.

Prayer Focus

1. **Blessing Your Legacy**: Speak God's promises over your children, grandchildren, and spiritual "children."

2. **Breaking Negative Cycles**: Ask the Holy Spirit to replace damaging family patterns with a fresh heritage of godliness.

Prayer

Lord, You have been faithful through every generation, and I trust You with mine. Today, I, _____, lift up my family—those here now and those yet to come. In Jesus' Name, I break every negative cycle that has tried to take root, and I declare blessings of salvation, peace, and integrity over my descendants. May they walk in Your favor, stand firm in Your truth, and flourish under Your grace. Amen.

Declaration

"My family line is marked by God's favor. I cancel any curses, declaring a legacy of faith, hope, and love for a thousand generations."

Day 20 – Mindful Meditation and Peaceful Reflection

Key Scripture

"But his delight is in the law of the Lord, and on his law he meditates day and night." *(Psalm 1:2)*

Devotional Thought

With the swirl of demands, noise, and rapid information around us, our minds often feel scattered. Yet the Word of God invites us into a place of calm and clarity. Through deliberate meditation on Scripture, we anchor ourselves in unchanging truth. In that stillness, we gain fresh perspective: God is bigger than every worry. As you habitually pause, reflect, and savor His Word, peace will guard your heart.

Prayer Focus

1. **Quieting the Mind**: Ask God for help in removing distractions so you can focus on His Word.
2. **Heart Transformation**: Pray that as you meditate, the Holy Spirit shapes your thoughts to mirror God's heart.

Prayer

Lord, in the midst of all the noise around me, draw me—_____—into the quiet streams of Your presence. Teach me to delight in Your Word, to meditate on Your truth day and night. Let every anxious thought in my mind be replaced by the unshakable promises You have spoken. Calm me, change me, and fill me with a peace that only You can give. In Jesus' Name, amen.

Declaration

"My mind is stilled by God's Word. As I meditate on His promises, peace, and wisdom become my portion."

Day 21 – Trials in Finances or Provision

Key Scripture

"And my God will meet all your needs according to the riches of his glory in Christ Jesus." *(Philippians 4:19)*

Devotional Thought

Financial strain can stir anxiety or shame, making us doubt God's care. But the Bible assures us our Provider has no shortage of resources. Sometimes, He leads us through humble seasons to teach trust and contentment. Other times, He blesses generously, equipping us to bless others. Wherever you stand, you can believe this: The Lord sees, the Lord knows, and the Lord provides.

Prayer Focus

1. **Trust in God's Supply**: Surrender any fear or anxiety about finances, believing in His provision.

2. **Wisdom & Stewardship**: Pray for divine guidance to manage resources responsibly and generously.

Prayer

Jehovah Jireh, my Provider, You see my needs even before I speak them. I, _____, lay my financial burdens before You, trusting in Your perfect provision. Teach me to rely on Your abundance, not my own efforts. Give me the discipline to manage what You've entrusted to me, the generosity to bless others, and the wisdom to recognize the doors You open. Let my life be a testimony of Your faithfulness. In Jesus' Name, amen.

Declaration

"My God is my Provider. Lack does not define me; I am blessed to be a blessing. I trust His timely provision."

Day 22 – Praying Through Impatience & Waiting on God

Key Scripture

"But those who wait on the Lord shall renew their strength..." *(Isaiah 40:31)*

Devotional Thought

Waiting is rarely comfortable. Impatience can creep in, tempting you to rush ahead of God's plan. Yet in the delay, God often does His greatest work in us— refining our character, growing our faith, and aligning our hearts with His will. Patience isn't passive; it's an active trust that God's timing is perfect. When you feel restless, lean deeper into Him, knowing that waiting on the Lord always yields a harvest of blessings.

Prayer Focus

1. **Surrender of Timelines**: Lay down your deadlines and trust God's perfect timing.

2. **Heart Refinement**: Ask God to shape your character during the waiting season.

Prayer

Father, forgive me for my impatience. I _____ confess that I often want quick fixes instead of trusting Your time and ways. As I wait, refine me. Strengthen my faith and deepen my intimacy with You. I believe You know exactly when and how to bring my breakthrough. Teach me to rest in Your sovereignty. In Christ's Name, amen.

Declaration

"I will not hurry ahead of God. His timing is flawless. I choose patient faith, confident that He is working all things for my good."

Day 23 – Protecting Your Home and Family

Key Scripture

"But as for me and my household, we will serve the Lord." *(Joshua 24:15)*

Devotional Thought

Your home is meant to be a place of refuge, love, and peace—a safe harbor from the storms of life. Spiritual warfare can target this sanctuary through conflicts, fear, or strife. Stand guard at your home's door through prayer. Invite God's presence to reign in every conversation, every decision, every routine. As you consistently declare that your household belongs to Him, the atmosphere shifts and God's protection becomes tangible.

Prayer Focus

1. **Spiritual Covering**: Ask God to surround your home with angelic protection and to fill it with His peace.

2. **Unity & Love**: Pray for hearts bound by love, forgiveness, and respect within your family.

Prayer

Lord, I _____ dedicate my home to You. May it be a place where Your presence dwells and Your truth is honored. Guard my family from any attack, whether spiritual or physical. Let the atmosphere of our home radiate love, joy, and peace. Together we choose to serve You wholeheartedly. In Jesus' precious Name, amen.

Declaration

"My home is covered by the blood of Jesus. Strife and darkness have no place here. We are a household that serves the Lord."

Day 24 – Heart Check: Pride vs. Humility

Key Scripture

"Humble yourselves before the Lord, and he will lift you up." *(James 4:10)*

Devotional Thought

In our quest for significance, pride can subtly creep in—highlighting our achievements, feeding self-reliance, or comparing us to others. Humility, however, acknowledges God as the true source of our worth and success. Embracing humility isn't self-loathing; it's recognizing that every talent, victory, and breath is a gift from God. When we humble ourselves, we create space for God's uplifting grace.

Prayer Focus

1. **Self-Examination**: Ask the Holy Spirit to reveal areas where pride has taken root.

2. **Grace & Growth**: Pray for a humble heart that welcomes correction, service, and dependence on the Lord.

Prayer

Lord, I repent of the pride that has crept into my heart—the times I've relied on my own strength or looked down on others. Teach me, _____, the beauty of true humility so that my life reflects the servant heart of Christ. Let my desires and ego fade as You take center stage within me. I trust You to lift me up in Your perfect time, for Your glory alone. In Jesus' Name, amen.

Declaration

"I lay down pride and choose humility. I rely on God's strength and wisdom, and He lifts me according to His purpose."

Day 25 – Battling Adultery and Affairs of the Heart

Key Scripture

"Marriage should be honored by all... for God will judge the adulterer..." *(Hebrews 13:4)*

Devotional Thought

Affairs don't start in the bedroom; they begin in the heart. Our culture normalizes flirtation, porn addiction, and emotional entanglements, yet these compromise the sacred covenant God established for marriage. If you're tempted, God provides a way of escape. If you've stumbled, His grace can redeem. Honor your vows by setting firm boundaries and continuously seeking God to guard your heart against compromise.

Prayer Focus

1. **Repentance & Cleansing**: If you've crossed lines, humbly repent and receive God's mercy.
2. **Holy Boundaries**: Ask God to protect your heart and mind, helping you remain faithful in thought and action.

Prayer

Lord, You designed marriage as a sacred bond, a reflection of Your unwavering love. I, _____, ask for Your forgiveness for any thoughts, desires, or actions that have fallen short of honoring this covenant. Wash me clean and renew my heart. Fill me with the strength to resist temptation and the wisdom to guard my commitment with firm boundaries. Let my marriage stand as a testimony to Your redeeming grace. In Jesus' Name, amen.

Declaration

"My marriage (or future marriage) is sacred. I refuse to entertain unfaithful thoughts or actions. By God's power, I walk in purity and honor."

Day 26 – Claiming Victory Over Self-Sabotage

Key Scripture

"The thief comes only to steal and kill and destroy; I have come that they may have life, and have it to the full." *(John 10:10)*

Devotional Thought

The enemy often doesn't need to sabotage us if he can lure us into sabotaging ourselves—through negative self-talk, procrastination, or destructive habits. Jesus intends for us to live abundantly, but we can undermine this reality by agreeing with lies that say, "I can't do this. I'll fail again." Recognize those patterns. Then renounce them, and consciously choose the abundant life Jesus offers.

Prayer Focus

1. **Self-Reflection**: Ask the Holy Spirit to show you ways you unconsciously hinder your own growth.
2. **Renewed Mindset**: Pray for courage to break unhealthy patterns, embracing Christ's victorious identity for you.

Prayer

Jesus, shine Your light on any self-sabotaging thoughts or habits that have taken root in me. If I, _____, have believed the enemy's lies, I turn away from them now. I choose to fill my mind with Your truth—the promise of abundant life. Strengthen me to walk in faith, discipline, and hope. Thank You for breaking every chain of self-defeat. I stand firm in the victory You have already won. Amen.

Declaration

"I break every cycle of self-sabotage. My life aligns with God's abundant purpose. I am victorious and fruitful in Christ."

Day 27 – Restoration in Broken Friendships

Key Scripture

"If it is possible, as far as it depends on you, live at peace with everyone." (Romans 12:18)

Devotional Thought

Friendships fracture through betrayal, misunderstandings, or drifting apart. Yet God values relationships deeply. He calls us to seek peace, to forgive, and, when possible, to restore. True reconciliation may take time, but it begins with a humble heart. Even if the other person remains distant, your role is to pray and remain open to healing. Let grace pave the way toward renewed unity.

Prayer Focus

1. **Healing & Wisdom**: Ask God for clarity— whether to reach out, to offer an apology, or to set boundaries.

2. **Supernatural Reconciliation**: Pray for God to do what only He can, softening hearts and rebuilding trust.

Prayer

Lord, You see the pain in my heart over friendships that have been strained or lost. If it is Your will, bring healing and restoration. Show me, _____, when to apologize, when to extend grace, and when to release what I cannot change. Take away any bitterness or pride that lingers in me. Let love rise where division once stood. In Jesus' restoring Name, amen.

Declaration

"My friendships are under God's authority. I release offense and invite divine healing. Where peace can dwell, I choose peace."

Day 28 – Standing Firm Against Spiritual Attacks

Key Scripture

"Therefore take up the whole armor of God, that you may be able to withstand in the evil day..." *(Ephesians 6:13)*

Devotional Thought

Spiritual attacks aren't always dramatic or obvious. They can be subtle whispers of doubt, discouragement, or conflict. Recognizing these tactics is half the battle. Equipping yourself daily with God's Word, prayer, and worship seals you in divine armor. Stand firm, knowing the One who is in you is greater than any foe. Never forget: when you stand in Jesus' authority, the enemy must flee.

Prayer Focus

1. **Daily Armor**: Ask for a renewed commitment to spiritual disciplines that keep your armor on.
2. **Vigilance**: Pray for heightened awareness to detect the enemy's schemes early and respond with truth.

Prayer

Mighty God, You have given me everything I need to stand strong in the battle. Today, I, _____, choose to put on the armor You have provided—the belt of truth to keep me grounded, the breastplate of righteousness to guard my heart, the gospel of peace to guide my steps, the shield of faith to extinguish every attack, the helmet of salvation to protect my mind, and the sword of the Spirit to stand on Your Word. Strengthen me to persevere, knowing that victory is already mine in Christ. Amen.

Declaration

"I am fully armed in God's strength. The devil's schemes fail against me. I stand firm, confident in Christ's triumph."

Day 29 – Worship as Warfare

Key Scripture

"As they began to sing and praise, the Lord set ambushes against the men... and they were defeated." *(2 Chronicles 20:21–22)*

Devotional Thought

When you choose to worship in the face of fear, opposition, or uncertainty, the enemy trembles. Praise magnifies God's presence and diminishes the roar of the battle. Worship forces your focus off the problem and onto the problem solver. It's not escapism— it's a deliberate weapon that shifts the atmosphere and welcomes God's power to move. Let your praise be a victory cry, declaring that God is enthroned above every challenge.

Prayer Focus

1. **Heart of Thanksgiving**: Begin each prayer time by thanking God for who He is, regardless of circumstances.

2. **Atmosphere Shift**: Ask the Holy Spirit to transform heaviness into joy as you praise.

Prayer

Lord, You are worthy of all my praise. In every battle I face, I, _____, choose to lift a song of thanksgiving. Teach me to worship with a heart anchored in spirit and truth, knowing that as I exalt You, the enemy's plans fall apart. Let my praise rise as a weapon that invites Your power into my situation. In Jesus' victorious Name, amen.

Declaration

"My worship is a weapon. When I praise God, the enemy is defeated. I fix my eyes on the King who is greater than any battle."

Day 30 – Living in Triumph and Joy

Key Scripture

"Do not grieve, for the joy of the Lord is your strength." *(Nehemiah 8:10)*

Devotional Thought

After thirty days of intentional prayer, reflection, and warfare, your spirit is attuned to the truth: we are fighting from victory, not for victory. Jesus secured triumph on the cross, and we participate in it by faith. Now is the time to rejoice. Joy isn't a fleeting emotion; it's a divine strength that rises above hardships. Let this journey propel you into a lifestyle of victory, anchored in God's unshakable love.

Prayer Focus

1. **Celebration**: Thank God for every breakthrough, every lesson learned, and every step of growth.

2. **Continual Reliance**: Commit to ongoing prayer and dependence on the Holy Spirit, even after these 30 days.

Prayer

Heavenly Father, I _____ celebrate the ground gained through this season of prayer. Thank You for every victory, every healing, every revelation. More than that, thank You for being my unchanging Savior. Let Your joy fill my heart daily. As I continue forward, I trust the Holy Spirit to keep me watchful, faithful, and triumphant. In Jesus' precious Name, amen.

Declaration

"I live in Christ's triumph. His joy is my strength. I move forward with hope, secured in God's unchanging grace."

Conclusion

You've come a long way in these thirty days of warfare prayers. Perhaps you've discovered strongholds you never knew existed, or you've finally found release from heaviness that weighed on your soul. Maybe you've seen doors swing wide open, or you're still waiting for answers—either way, take a moment to celebrate the miracles. Sometimes the greatest breakthrough is peace of mind or a softened heart. Write down every shift—small or large—because testimonies from past battles fuel faith for the future.

Remember the words of Dr. Billy Graham: *Never stop praying, no matter how dark and hopeless your case may seem.* God *is* moving. Even if all you see right now is a tiny flicker of hope, fan that flame with thanksgiving. As you look back, ask yourself: What lies did the enemy once whisper that no longer have a hold on you? In what ways has your trust in God deepened? These reflections anchor you in God's faithfulness.

Moving Forward in Victory

Spiritual warfare isn't a single round of prayer—it's a lifestyle. The enemy thrives on discouragement, distractions, and delays, but you hold the secret weapon: perseverance. On days you feel strong, pray boldly. On days you stumble, pick yourself up and pray anyway. If you miss a day or two (or ten!), don't let the accuser's lies keep you down. *Begin again.* There is no such thing as permanent failure in God's kingdom—only new mercies every morning.

Put on your armor daily (Ephesians 6:10–18). Remember, your shield of faith can quench *all* the fiery darts of the enemy. Keep saturating your spirit with God's Word, for it's the sword that cuts through every lie. And never lose sight of the unstoppable truth: **He who is in you is greater than he who is in the world** (1 John 4:4).

Appendix

Additional Scriptures for Ongoing Warfare

- **Deuteronomy 20:1**—God is with you no matter how intimidating the battle looks.

- **Psalm 46:1–2**—He is your refuge and strength, an ever-present help in trouble.

- **Isaiah 54:17**—No weapon formed against you shall prosper.

- **2 Corinthians 10:3–5**—Tear down every stronghold by bringing thoughts into obedience to Christ.

- **James 4:7**—Submit to God, resist the devil, and watch him flee.

- **1 Peter 5:8–9**—Be vigilant; your adversary prowls, but you can resist him, firm in faith.

- **Romans 8:31**—If God is for you, who can be against you?

Suggested Worship Songs & Spiritual Reading

1. **Worship Songs**
   - *"See a Victory"* by Elevation Worship
   - *"This Is How I Fight My Battles (Surrounded)"* by Upper Room
   - *"No Longer Slaves"* by Bethel Music
   - *"What a Beautiful Name"* by Hillsong Worship

2. **Books & Devotionals**
   - *Victory in Spiritual Warfare* by Dr. Tony Evans
   - *Spiritual Warfare for Women* by Leighann McCoy

- *101 Tactics for Spiritual Warfare* by Jennifer LeClaire
- **Journaling Pages / Reflection Questions**

Use these prompts to keep your prayer life vibrant:

1. **Daily Praise**: What's one characteristic of God you've experienced today—His faithfulness, kindness, or protection?
2. **Battles & Breakthroughs**: Identify current spiritual struggles. How has God spoken to you about them?
3. **Answered Prayers**: Document ways God has shown up. No testimony is too small.
4. **Continued Warfare Plan**: Are there specific Scriptures or prayer strategies you need to revisit?
5. **New Mercies**: Where do you need a fresh start in your prayer life? How will you *begin again*?

Sister, our walk with God is not about never falling—it's about getting back up, time and time again, clothed in His grace and armed with fervent prayer. As you close this chapter of focused warfare, step into your next season with bold expectancy. **You are a daughter of the King—loved, chosen, and empowered.** The enemy may prowl, but his threats pale in comparison to the Lion of Judah who roars on your behalf.

Go forth in peace, confidence, and unshakeable faith. Keep praying. Keep standing. Keep shining. And remember: every time your knees hit the ground in prayer, the powers of darkness tremble, because the battle is the Lord's—and in Christ, you are already victorious.

Amen and amen.

www.ingramcontent.com/pod-product-compliance
Lightning Source LLC
Chambersburg PA
CBHW061704120626
46550CB00003B/1084